CHECK YOUR NECK

more of You Might Be A Redneck If...

JEFF FOXWORTHY

Illustrations by David Boyd

LONGSTREET PRESS
Atlanta, Georgia

For the newest girl and love in my life,
my daughter Jordan

Published by
LONGSTREET PRESS, INC.
A subsidiary of Cox Newspapers,
A subsidiary of Cox Enterprises, Inc.
2140 Newmarket Parkway
Suite 122
Marietta, GA 30067

Printed in the United States of America

13th printing, 1997

Library of Congress Catalog Number 92-71790

ISBN 1-56352-048-6

This book was printed by Data Reproductions Corporation, Rochester Hills, Michigan.
The text was set in Palatino.
Cover illustration by David Boyd. Cover design by Jill Dible.
Part of YOU MIGHT BE A REDNECK IF ... series by Jeff Foxworthy

Foreword

Well, this is the third book in the *You Might Be a Redneck If . . .* series, and I still get asked all the time, "What is a Redneck?" I guess the easiest answer is that Redneck is an unsophisticated state of mind. What's more, I've found that almost everyone qualifies to some extent. Lord knows, I'm guilty of more than a few of the 150 examples found in each book. After all, how do you think I know about this stuff?

People come up to me all the time at book signings and say, "I'm not a Redneck, but I have a brother who is." I don't even look up. I just hand them a book and say, "Start reading." Sure enough, after a few pages they'll say, "Oh my God, I've done that!" On the other hand, I've had folks proudly announce that they thought the book was their autobiography. The point is, there are full-time and part-time Rednecks, and most of us know where we fall on the scale.

If you're still confused or distressed about what shade of red your neck might be, you worry too much. Learn to laugh at yourself, hopefully using my books, and grade yourself against the following scorecard:

Out of 150 examples, if you're guilty of . . .

0 —	I hope your butler runs off with your silverware.
1-2 —	Don't take it personally, but you're probably a boring, arrogant snob.
3-5 —	You need to have more fun.
6-10 —	I bet you keep these books on the back of your toilet.
11-20 —	Didn't we meet at the state fair?
21-40 —	I'll see you at the family reunion.
41-75 —	How much do you want for that stove in your front yard?
76-100 —	You've seen Elvis recently, haven't you?
101-125 —	Come get your goat out of my yard.
126-149 —	Nice tooth!
150 —	Who read this book to you?

Keep Laughing,
Jeff Foxworthy

You might be a redneck if . . .

You ever cut your grass and found a car.

– ✧ –

You own a home that is mobile and
five cars that aren't.

– ✧ –

You think the stock market has
a fence around it.

You might be a redneck if . . .

Your stereo speakers used to belong to the
Moonlight Drive-in Theater.

– ✧ –

You've ever lost a loved one to kudzu.

– ✧ –

Your boat has not left the driveway in
15 years.

You might be a redneck if . . .

You've ever shot anyone for looking at you.

You might be a redneck if . . .

You own a homemade fur coat.

– ◈ –

Chiggers are included on your list of top
five hygiene concerns.

– ◈ –

You burn your front yard rather than
mow it.

You might be a redneck if . . .

Any of your children were conceived in a car wash.

You might be a redneck if . . .

Your wife has ever said, "Come move this transmission so I can take a bath."

– ✧ –

You refer to the time you won a free case of motor oil as "the day my ship came in."

– ✧ –

You read the Auto Trader with a highlight pen.

You might be a redneck if . . .

The Salvation Army declines your mattress.

You might be a redneck if . . .

You own all the components of soap on a
rope except the soap.

– ✧ –

You've ever raked leaves in your kitchen.

– ✧ –

Your entire family has ever sat around
waiting for a call from the governor
to spare a loved one.

You might be a redneck if . . .

Your grandmother has ever been asked
to leave a bingo game because of
her language.

– ✧ –

Someone asks, "Where's your bowling
bag?" and you answer, "She's at
home with the kids."

– ✧ –

When describing your kids, you use the
phrase "dumb as a brick."

You might be a redneck if . . .

Birds are attracted to your beard.

You might be a redneck if . . .

Your wife's job requires her to wear
an orange vest.

– ✧ –

You were shooting pool when any of
your children were born.

– ✧ –

You have the local taxidermist's
number on speed dial.

You might be a redneck if . . .

You've ever hit a deer with your car ...
deliberately.

– ✧ –

Your school fight song was
"Dueling Banjos."

– ✧ –

You think a chain saw is a musical
instrument.

You might be a redneck if . . .

You've ever held up someone with a caulk gun.

You might be a redneck if . . .

You've ever attended a dance at the
bus station.

– ✧ –

You've ever given rat traps as a gift.

– ✧ –

You swapped a set of tires for your
wife's wedding ring.

You might be a redneck if . . .

You've ever
stolen clothes
from a scarecrow.

You might be a redneck if . . .

The most common phrase heard in your house is, "Somebody go jiggle the handle."

– ✧ –

You always answer the door with a baseball bat in your hand.

– ✧ –

You clean your fingernails with a stick.

You might be a redneck if . . .

You secretly get your firewood from
your neighbor's yard.

– ✧ –

Your coffee table used to be a telephone
cable spool.

– ✧ –

You keep a can of Raid on the
kitchen table.

You might be a redneck if . . .

You've ever used a toilet seat as a picture frame.

You might be a redneck if . . .

Your Christmas tree is still up in February.

– ✧ –

You've ever been arrested for loitering.

– ✧ –

You hammer bottle caps into the frame of
your front door to make it look nice.

You might be a redneck if . . .

Your wife can climb a tree faster than
your cat.

– ✧ –

You own a pair of cut-offs made from
double-knit pants.

– ✧ –

Your mother has "ammo" on
her Christmas list.

You might be a redneck if . . .

Every socket in your house breaks a fire code.

You might be a redneck if . . .

You've totaled every car you've ever owned.

– ✧ –

There are more than five McDonald's bags currently in the floorboard of your car.

– ✧ –

Mama taught you how to "flip" a cigarette.

You might be a redneck if . . .

You've never paid for a haircut.

You might be a redneck if . . .

There is a wasp nest in your living room.

– ✧ –

The Home Shopping Club operator
recognizes your voice.

– ✧ –

You think the traffic sign "MERGE" is
a personal challenge.

You might be a redneck if . . .

You give your dad a gallon of Pepto-Bismol for his birthday.

– ✧ –

There has ever been crime-scene tape on your bathroom door.

– ✧ –

You've ever been kicked out of the zoo for heckling the monkeys.

You might be a redneck if . . .

You take your dog for a walk and you both use the same tree at the corner.

You might be a redneck if . . .

The taillight covers of your car are
made of tape.

– ✧ –

Your car has never had a full tank of gas.

– ✧ –

Your mother has ever been involved
in a "cuss fight" with the high
school principal.

You might be a redneck if . . .

You've ever worn shorts to a funeral home.

You might be a redneck if . . .

You think a subdivision is part of a
math problem.

– ◇ –

You've ever bathed with flea and tick soap.

– ◇ –

Your good deed for the month was hiding
your brother for a few days.

You might be a redneck if . . .

Your wheelbarrow breaks and it takes
three relatives to figure out how to fix it.

– ✧ –

You think "taking out the trash" means
taking your in-laws to a movie.

– ✧ –

You have every episode of "Hee-Haw"
on tape.

You might be a redneck if . . .

Your mama tore her best dress coon hunting.

You might be a redneck if . . .

You've ever been involved in a custody
fight over a hunting dog.

– ✧ –

You're considered an expert on
worm beds.

– ✧ –

You own a pair of knee-high moccasins.

You might be a redneck if . . .

Your kids take a siphon hose to "Show and Tell."

You might be a redneck if . . .

The dog catcher calls for a back-up unit
when visiting your house.

– ✧ –

The flood history of your area can be seen
on your living room walls.

– ✧ –

You haul more than U-Haul.

You might be a redneck if . . .

Your mother has ever stomped into the
house and announced, "The feud
is back on!"

– ✧ –

Your most recent business improvement
was repainting your "Garage Sale" sign.

– ✧ –

Your wedding was held in the
delivery room.

You might be a redneck if . . .

You've ever bought a used cap.

You might be a redneck if . . .

Your soap on a rope doubles as an
air freshener.

– ✧ –

Your wife's hairdo attracts bees.

– ✧ –

Your baby's first words are, "Attention,
Kmart shoppers."

You might be a redneck if . . .

You've ever shot a deer from inside your house.

You might be a redneck if . . .

Your C.B. antenna is a danger to
low-flying planes.

– ✧ –

Your primary source of income is
the pawn shop.

– ✧ –

In an effort to watch your cholesterol,
you start eating Spam Lite.

You might be a redneck if . . .

You pick your teeth from a catalog.

– ✧ –

Your masseuse uses lard.

– ✧ –

You can't take a nap without at least one
hand tucked inside your pants.

You might be a redneck if . . .

Your favorite
T-shirt is declared
offensive in 13
states.

You might be a redneck if . . .

You attend a parent-teacher conference
wearing flip-flops.

– ✧ –

You think Long John Silver is
formal underwear.

– ✧ –

Your wife's best shoes have steel toes.

You can entertain yourself for more than
an hour with a fly swatter.

You might be a redneck if . . .

You've ever financed a tattoo.

– ✧ –

You've ever used a laundromat as a mailing address.

– ✧ –

You use a fishing license as a form of I.D.

You might be a redneck if . . .

Your stomach is
bigger than any
shirt you own.

Your grandmother knows how to correctly
execute the "sleeper hold."

You might be a redneck if . . .

On stag night, you take a real deer.

– ✧ –

You use a '55 Chevy as a guest house.

– ✧ –

Your back porch is bigger than your house.

You might be a redneck if . . .

You've ever stolen
toilet paper.

You might be a redneck if . . .

There is more oil in your baseball cap
than in your car.

– ◇ –

Your deceased hunting dog's tombstone is
larger than your grandfather's.

– ◇ –

You think a hot tub is a stolen
bathroom fixture.

You might be a redneck if . . .

A full-grown ostrich has fewer feathers
than your cowboy hat.

– ✧ –

You can't understand why there are no
tuxedos made of flannel.

– ✧ –

An expired license plate means another
decoration for your living room wall.

You might be a redneck if . . .

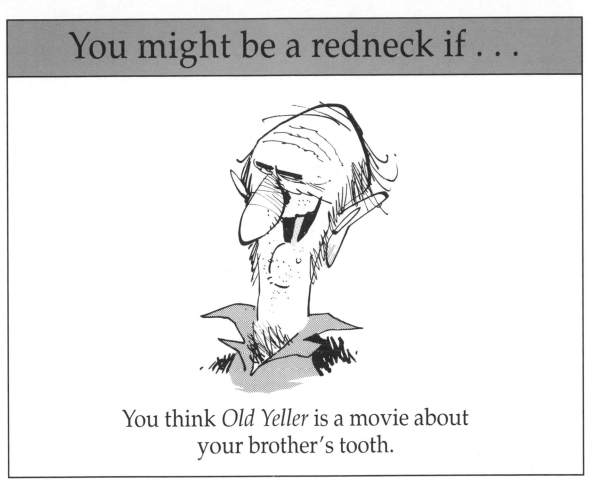

You think *Old Yeller* is a movie about
your brother's tooth.

You might be a redneck if . . .

You watch "Little House on the Prairie"
for decorating tips.

– ✧ –

Your secret family recipe is illegal.

– ✧ –

Your handkerchief doubles as your
shirt sleeve.

You might be a redneck if . . .

Your kid's favorite teething ring is the
garden hose in the front yard.

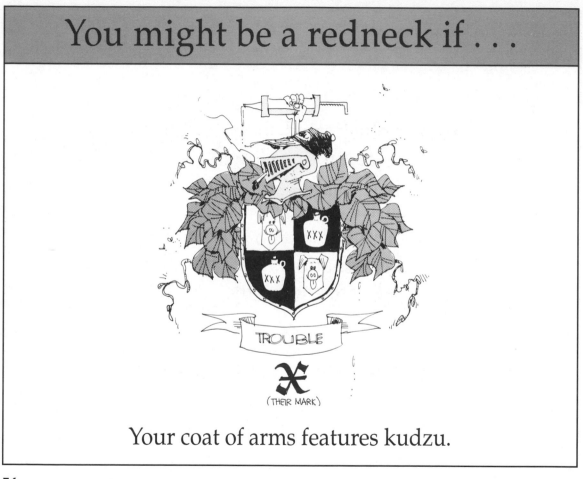

Your coat of arms features kudzu.

You might be a redneck if . . .

Your sophisticated show-biz cousin
is a rodeo clown.

– ✧ –

You think people who send out high
school graduation announcements
are show-offs.

– ✧ –

Your best ashtray is a turtle shell.

You might be a redneck if . . .

Your pocketknife has ever been
referred to as "Exhibit A."

You might be a redneck if . . .

You think cur is a breed of dog.

– ◇ –

People hear your car a long time
before they see it.

– ◇ –

The man from the power company
threatens to cut off your service, and you
threaten to cut off something of
his in return.

You might be a redneck if . . .

Your four-year-old is a member of
the NRA.

– ✧ –

Your satellite dish payment delays buying
back-to-school clothes for the kids.

– ✧ –

Your most expensive shoes have
numbers on the heels.

Your wife has
ever burned out
an electric razor.

You might be a redneck if . . .

Your birth announcement included
the words "rug rat."

– ◇ –

You've ever hitchhiked naked.

– ◇ –

You're turned on by a woman who can
field dress a deer.

You might be a redneck if . . .

You use the "O" on the stop sign in front of
your house to sight your new rifle.

You might be a redneck if . . .

Your Christmas cards have a Xerox copy
of your butt included.

– ✧ –

Your bumper sticker says, "My other car
is a combine."

– ✧ –

The gas pedal on your car is shaped
like a bare foot.

You might be a redneck if . . .

Your screen door
has no screen.

You might be a redneck if . . .

The highlight of your parties is when you
flip out your false teeth.

You might be a redneck if . . .

Your wife keeps a can of Vienna sausage
in her purse.

– ✧ –

You prefer car keys to Q-tips.

– ✧ –

Taking a dip has nothing to do with water.

You might be a redneck if . . .

There are more than 10 lawsuits currently
pending against your dog.

You might be a redneck if . . .

You take a fishing pole into Sea World.

– ✧ –

The hood and one door are a different
color from the rest of your car.

– ✧ –

You've ever filled your deer tag on
the golf course.

You might be a redneck if . . .

You've ever shot someone over a mall
parking space.

– ✧ –

Santa Claus refuses to let your kids
sit in his lap.

– ✧ –

Your toilet paper has page numbers on it.

You might be a redneck if . . .

You think mud wrestling should be an Olympic sport.

People are
scared to touch
your bathrobe.

You might be a redneck if . . .

The receptionist is responsible for checking
the rat traps at your place of business.

– ✧ –

You list your parole officer as a reference.

– ✧ –

There are more fish on your walls
than pictures.

You might be a redneck if . . .

Motel 6 turns off the lights when they see you coming.

You might be a redneck if . . .

There are more dishes in your sink than
in your cabinets.

– ✧ –

You think a turtleneck is a key ingredient
to soup.

– ✧ –

At the dog track, you always bet on the
dog that "does his business" right
before the race starts.

You might be a redneck if . . .

You fainted when you met Slim Whitman.

You might be a redneck if . . .

You've ever stood in line to have your picture made with a freak of nature.

– ✧ –

Your anniversary present was getting the septic tank pumped.

– ✧ –

Your local ambulance has a trailer hitch.

You might be a redneck if . . .

You watch cartoons long after your kids become bored.

– ✧ –

You think the French Riviera is a foreign car.

– ✧ –

You consider yourself an entrepreneur because of the "Dirt for Sale" sign in your front yard.